Rookie
Read-About® Math

Grouping at the Dog Show

By Simone T. Ribke

Consultants

Chalice Bennett
Elementary Specialist
Martin Luther King Jr. Laboratory School
Evanston, Illinois

Ari Ginsburg
Math Curriculum Specialist

Children's Press®
A Division of Scholastic Inc.
New York   Toronto   London   Auckland   Sydney
Mexico City   New Delhi   Hong Kong
Danbury, Connecticut

Designer: Herman Adler Design
Photo Researcher: Caroline Anderson
The photo on the cover shows three shih tzu (SHEET-su) dogs.

Library of Congress Cataloging-in-Publication Data

Ribke, Simone T.
  Grouping at the dog show / by Simone T. Ribke.
    p. cm. — (Rookie read-about math)
  ISBN 0-516-24959-2 (lib. bdg.)   0-516-28100-3 (pbk.)
  1. Set theory—Juvenile literature. I. Title. II. Series.
  QA248.R48 2006
  511.3'22—dc22
                                        2005019971

CHILDREN'S PRESS, and ROOKIE READ-ABOUT®,
and associated logos are trademarks and/or registered trademarks
of Scholastic Library Publishing. SCHOLASTIC and associated logos
are trademarks and/or registered trademarks of Scholastic Inc.

1 2 3 4 5 6 7 8 9 10 R 15 14 13 12 11 10 09 08 07 06

Today is the dog show!

There are many groups
of dogs to see.

Handlers groom the dogs before the show. Grooming is washing and brushing the dogs.

These dogs are waiting
to be groomed.

Some have ears that
stand up. Some have ears
that hang down.

The group of dogs with
ears that stand up will be
groomed first. Which dogs
will be groomed second?

You can use a diagram
(DYE-uh-gram) to
help you.

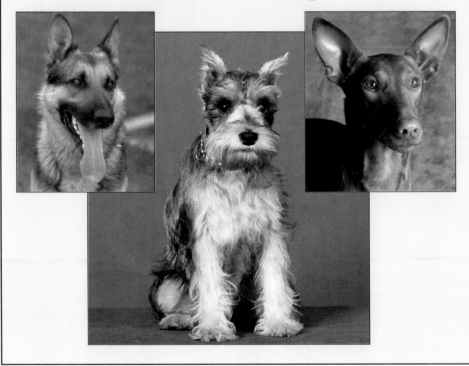

GROOMED FIRST
Ears that Stand Up

The group of dogs with
ears that hang down will
be groomed second.

GROOMED SECOND
Ears that Hang Down

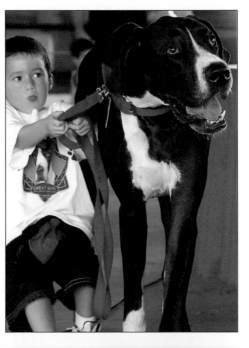

The smallest dogs at the show are called "toy" dogs.

How many of these dogs are part of the toy group?

Four of these dogs are part of the toy group.

Toy Dogs

Not Toy Dogs

14

These dogs have jobs.

The dogs in this group help farmers herd sheep or cows.

This group is called the herding group.

Which of these herding dogs have smooth coats?

All the dogs in the
rectangle are herding dogs.

Herding dogs with smooth
coats are shown inside
the circle.

The herding dog with a
curly coat is shown inside
the rectangle, but outside
the circle.

HERDING DOGS

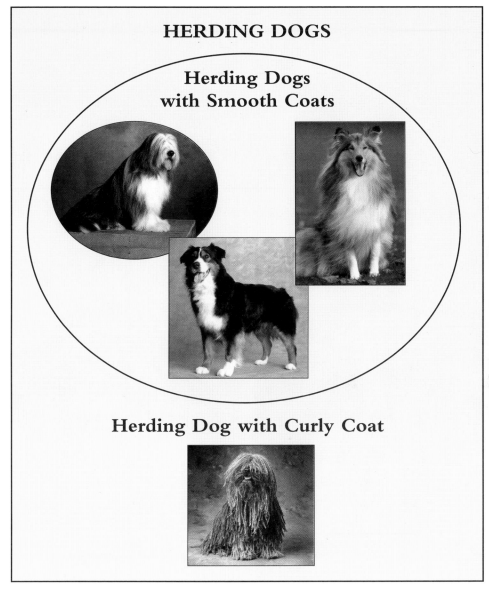

Herding Dogs
with Smooth Coats

Herding Dog with Curly Coat

18

A dog's muzzle (MUH-zuhl) is its nose and mouth. A muzzle can be short or long.

Which dogs belong to the group with short muzzles?

Which dogs belong to the group with long muzzles?

Use the diagram to learn how many dogs are in each group.

Are there more dogs with short muzzles or long muzzles?

Short Muzzles

Long Muzzles

There are more dogs with short muzzles.

The dogs in this group have coats that are short or red.

How many dogs have coats that are both short and red?

A diagram like this
one can help you find
the answer.

One dog in the group
has a coat that is short
and red.

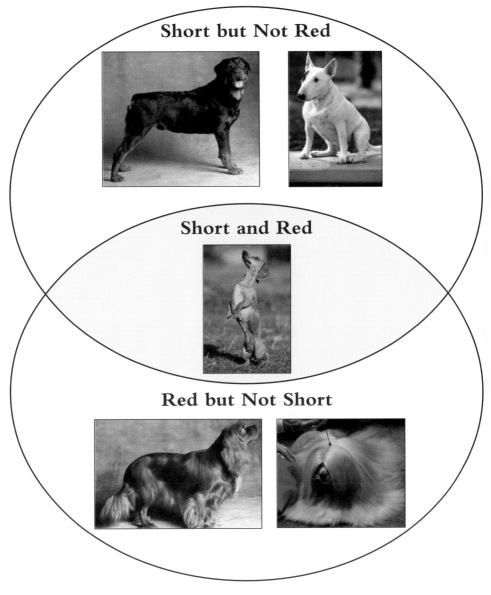

Short but Not Red

Short and Red

Red but Not Short

The judges call a group of dogs into the show ring. It is time to pick the winner.

The winner has a short tail. It has a short coat. It has ears that stand up.

Which dog is the winner? Turn the page to find out.

This dog is the winner!

It's fun to group dogs at the dog show!

Words You Know

ears

groom

group

herding dog

30

muzzle

tail

toy dog

winner

Index

About the Author

Simone T. Ribke is a writer and editor of children's books. Since earning a B.S. in elementary education, she has written a wide array of children's and professional educational materials, including work on a national math education program.

Photo Credits

Photographs © 2006: AP/Wide World Photos: 4, 5, 30 bottom left, 30 top right (Mary Altaffer), 3 (Joey Gardner), 10 top right, 13 top (Dylan Moore/The Potomac News); Corbis Images: 14 top left, 17 top left, 26 bottom right, 26 top right (Yann Arthus-Bertrand), 14 top right, 17 top right (Markus Botzeck/zefa), 7 bottom left, 8 center, 30 top left (Gary W. Carter), 7 center left, 9 top left, 14 bottom right, 17 center 18 top, 21 top, 22 center left, 25 top left, 26 left, 26 center, 26 bottom, 30 bottom right, 31 top (Robert Dowling), 10 top center, 12 top right (Ian Hodgson/Reuters), 22 bottom left, 25 bottom right (Karen Huntt), 10 bottom right, 12 bottom left, 31 bottom right (Matthew Klein), 7 bottom right, 9 bottom left (Paul A. Souders), 18 bottom right, 21 bottom left (Franco Vogt); Dembinsky Photo Assoc./Bonnie Nance: 18 bottom left, 21 center left; Getty Images: 18 center right, 21 bottom right (Arthur S. Aubry), 10 bottom left, 13 bottom (Robert Daley/Stone), 29, 31 bottom right (Sean Murphy/Stone); ImageState/Robert Dowling: 7 center right, 7 top right, 8 right, 9 right, 22 top left, 25 bottom left; Peter Arnold Inc./Patrice Beriault: 10 center left, 12 bottom right; Photo Researchers, NY/William H Mullins: 7 top left, 8 left; PhotoEdit/Deborah Davis: 22 top right, 25 top right; Superstock, Inc.: 14, bottom left, 17 bottom center, 22 bottom right, 25 center (age fotostock), cover (Bob Shirtz), 10 top left, 12 top left.

What Do You See in a Cloud?

By Allan Fowler

Consultants

Robert L. Hillerich, Professor Emeritus,
Bowling Green State University, Bowling Green, Ohio;
Consultant, Pinellas County Schools, Florida

Lynne Kepler, Educational Consultant

Fay Robinson, Child Development Specialist

Children's Press®
A Division of Grolier Publishing
New York   London   Hong Kong   Sydney
Danbury, Connecticut

Project Editor: Downing Publishing Services
Designer: Herman Adler Design Group
Photo Researcher: Feldman & Associates, Inc.

Library of Congress Cataloging-in-Publication Data

Fowler, Allan.
    What do you see in a cloud? / by Allan Fowler.
      p. cm. – (Rookie read-about science)
    Includes index.
    Summary: Simple text and illustrations describe what clouds are
made of, how they differ, and why they fall back to earth as rain.
    ISBN 0-516-06056-2 (lib. bdg.) – ISBN 0-516-20222-7 (pbk.)
    1. Clouds—Juvenile literature. [1. Clouds.] I. Title. II. Series.
QC921.35.F69   1996
551.57'6–dc20   95-39676
                                                 CIP
                                                  AC

You can see all kinds of
things when you look up
at clouds. One cloud could
be shaped like a fish . . .

another like a dog . . .

and another might remind
you of a spaceship.

What do you see in *this* cloud?

Clouds often seem to be in a hurry. The wind blows them across the sky.

One moment you're touched
by the shadow of a cloud —

and a moment later you're
in bright sunshine.

Rain comes from clouds.

In fact, clouds are made
of water.

Every day a great amount
of water rises into the air
from oceans, rivers, lakes
— even from the leaves
of plants and trees.

It rises in the form of very tiny drops called water vapor.

You can't see water vapor, but it's all around you.

The water vapor cools off as it rises, or meets cold air, or passes over cold land or water.

When the water vapor has cooled enough, the droplets come together and make clouds.

Have you ever seen your breath in front of your face on a winter day?

Then you actually saw a small cloud being formed as your warm, moist breath reached the cold air.

15

As the droplets in a cloud get cooler, they run together and make bigger drops — big enough now to fall back to earth as rain.

If the weather is cold
enough, the drops of water
freeze and fall as snow.

Clouds that are puffy
like cotton are called
cumulus clouds.

When cumulus clouds pile up like this, a thunderstorm may be coming.

Stratus clouds stretch across the sky in flat sheets.

Dark stratus clouds often bring rain.

Cirrus clouds are thin,
wispy, and high in the sky.

Clouds that form just above the ground are called fog. Sometimes a fog is so thick, you can't see the other side of the street.

This is what it looks like when you fly in a plane above a layer of clouds.

You see the sun shining on the clouds. But people on the ground can't see the sun.

To them, it's just another cloudy day.

You might like
sunny days better
than cloudy ones.

But without clouds, there would be no rain.

Without rain, nothing
could grow — and
you'd have nothing
to eat.

So you can be glad
there are rain clouds —
as long as you don't
forget your umbrella.

29

Words You Know

rain

snow

cloud

30

cirrus cloud

cumulus cloud

stratus cloud

fog

31

Index

About the Author

Allan Fowler is a free-lance writer with a background in advertising. Born in New York, he lives in Chicago now and enjoys traveling.

Photo Credits

Valan Photos — ©Harold V. Green, cover; ©Ken Patterson, 8, 9; ©J.R. Page, 11
©John Elk III, 3
H. Armstrong Roberts — ©H. Abernathy, 4
Tom Stack & Associates — ©Bob Pool, 5; ©Thomas Kitchin, 17, 30 (top right)
Photo Edit — ©Rhoda Sidney, 6; ©David Young-Wolff, 15; ©Myrleen Ferguson, 26
Visuals Unlimited — ©Steve McCutcheon, 7; ©A.J. Copley, 21; ©Walt Anderson, 27, 30 (bottom)
Tony Stone Images, Inc. — ©Scott Dietrich, 12; ©Darryl Torckler, 20, 31 (bottom left); ©Steve Elmore, 25
Earth Scenes — ©Joe McDonald, 16; ©John Lemker, 22, 31 (top left)
Root Resources — ©Louise K. Broman, 18, 31 (top right)
David G. Houser — ©Jan Butchofsky-Houser, 19
SuperStock International, Inc. — ©D.C. Lowe, 23, 31 (bottom right)
Photri, Inc. — 29, 30 (top left)
COVER: Cumulus cloud